BE HAPPY, B*TCH

A WORKBOOK BY TIFF REAGAN

DEDICATION:

This one is for myself.

YOU DESERVE TO BE HAPPY!

You may not feel like it right now, but you do. Trust me when I say that I know what it's like. I've been there. I made this workbook because I hate the sickly sweet, unrealistic, "good vibes" crap that self help is sometimes condensed to. If that is your thing, neat! But you picked up this title, so I'm going to go out on a limb here and assume you need a little more substance. Positive quotes are nice but they don't mean anything without action backing them up.

Can these exercises help you feel happier?
Hell yeah! It's called science, you beautiful bitch.

If you want to get out of a funk, this workbook can help. Or if you have clinical depression like me, this shit can become part of your routine. It's up to you! However you choose to use this book and these tools, remember that healing doesn't happen over night. Also, don't forget that you are a badass for working through your pain. You should celebrate that effort. Go on!

With gratitude,

Tiff Reagan

This workbook has two rules:

1. Be **honest** with yourself
2. Be **patient** with yourself

Get your ass back to happiness and positivity!

HERE'S WHAT WE'RE GOING TO COVER:

ARE **YOU** REA**DY, BITCH?**

YOU ARE WONDERFUL, EVEN WHEN YOU'RE HURTING

First thing is first, bitch -- feeling negative emotions does not mean you are weak, irrational, pathetic, or a failure. Get that bullshit out of your head.

If you are feeling down, depressed, angry, lonely, pessimistic, anxious, grim, melancholy, bitter, or another negative emotion, you are not broken. These emotions are completely normal.

In fact, they are really important signals that something is going on. Don't ignore what your body and brain are trying to tell you. Those signals are saying, "Hey, you have some unmet emotional needs."

They might also be signals of a health issue, like mental illness.

AND YOU'RE A LOT MORE NORMAL THAN YOU THINK

Of course you're special or whatever, but you are not abnormal. Since the 1930s, rates of depression and anxiety have been steadily increasing.

- More than 300 million people around the world suffer from depression.
- More than 18% of the population is affected by anxiety.

(Source: World Health Organization)

See, you're not alone. And you don't have to go at it alone, either. Be open with your loved ones about how you're feeling. If you have been feeling symptoms for a while, talk to your doctor or counselor.

1

SELF AWARE
AS **FUCK**

Start where you are

What is today's date? _____

Who are you, exactly? _____

How young are you? _____

What do you hope to get out of this workbook?

_____

_____

_____

Describe what your life is like in six words:

_____ _____ _____

_____ _____ _____

HOW ARE YOU FEELING, BITCH?

	The worst	Meh	The best
MOOD			
ENERGY			
HEALTH			
CAREER			
FINANCES			
GROWTH			
FAMILY			
LOVE LIFE			
SOCIAL			

What's a typical day off like?

MORNING

AFTERNOON

EVENING

Imagine that someone who hasn't met you yet sees the breakdown of your day. Take some time to think about what that day says about you.

- Is it filled with what brings you joy?
- Does it reflect who you really are?

Where you spend your time and energy should be a direct indicator of what you value.

CIRCLE ALL THE WORDS THAT DESCRIBE YOU

Flexible	Perceptive	Independent	Punctual	Thoughtful
Honest	Patient	Open-minded	Creative	Meticulous
Ambitious	Kind	Self-confident	Organized	Inventive
Energetic	Proactive	Charismatic	Hard-working	Responsible
Supportive	Funny	Analytical	Reliable	Articulate
Curious	Artistic	Empathetic	Intellectual	Cheerful

Having trouble? How would a good friend describe you?

CIRCLE ALL THE THINGS THAT YOU LOVE TO DO

Listening to people	Cheering someone up	Helping make decisions
Researching information	Taking care of animals	Writing
Teaching	Learning something new	Organizing objects
Fixing or building things	Telling stories	Talking in front of people
Coming up with strategies	Coordinating people	Explaining complex ideas
Giving advice	Creating arts or crafts	Coaching
Organizing information	Selling things	Taking care of children
Designing	Helping solve problems	Organizing events or parties

EXPLORE YOUR STRENGTHS

Look at what you circled on the previous pages. Pick three from each group. If you did not see your descriptor or action on the lists, write it in below.

Which three words best describe you?

Which three actions do you love the most?

These should reflect your strengths and your passions. When you're spending your time using strengths, you feel happier and more productive.

Think about a dream job that combines the three things you love to do and your three best qualities. What could you excel at?

Now, think about how to use your strengths in your current world. How can you use them in the job you have right now, at school, in your community, or in your social circle? Make a list.

Write your strengths down where you can see them every day.

Keeping them at the top of your mind will help guide you.

SKEPTICAL?

What if none of those things make sense and you feel super shitty about all of this? That's OK. Try new things. Ask to join friends in their hobbies. Create a list of what makes you different than other people. Your strengths will start to shine through. Also, consider taking a personal strengths test.

NOTES ABOUT STRENGTHS

WHO ARE YOU SPENDING YOUR TIME WITH?

We all have negative people in our lives. But did you know that negativity can be contagious and harm your health? It can cause stress, anxiety, heart disease, poor immune function, and it can even rewire your brain.

Limit your interactions with negative people. They are toxic and won't help your journey to happiness. Say goodbye to those assholes!

SURROUND YOURSELF WITH PEOPLE WHO ARE OPTIMISTIC, POSITIVE, PRODUCTIVE, AND HAPPY.

WHO DO YOU ADMIRE?

Think about two people you admire and respect. What makes them special?

	Person 1	Person 2
Who is it?		
In your eyes, what are their best qualities?		
What qualities do you have in common?		

Conversation not comparison

Instead of comparing yourself to someone you admire, be proactive and ask them to hang out.

Have a conversation with them. Go deep.

- Tell them what you admire about them.
- Ask about their philosophy on life.
- Ask them what they do to maintain good mental health.
- Find out what happiness is to them.

Start building a bond and a stronger connection based on honesty and vulnerability. You will find that you have more in common than you previously believed.

CONVERSATION NOTES & IDEAS

We all make choices about the information we share with each other. People are natural storytellers and natural story editors. We pick what's important and relevant, and then leave out the unnecessary details.

When we are unhappy, we focus on the negative. We choose to describe ourselves in the harshest light and find details or events in our past to reinforce our feelings. That's confirmation bias.

But what if we looked at our lives and decided to tell a different story? If we interpret our difficult moments in a more positive way, we can change how we see ourselves. Let's try it!

CONTROL YOUR OWN STORY

WHAT STORIES DO YOU TELL ABOUT YOURSELF?

By controlling your story, you can turn failure into personal growth and learning opportunities. Talk about a hard breakup as a chance to understand what you want in a relationship, instead of a tragedy. What if getting fired or flunking a class was a motivator or a life lesson, instead of an example of inadequacy?

Pick two stories and rewrite them.

My negative story	A more positive version

What story do you want other people to tell?

Put yourself in the shoes of a person you admire. How do you want to be described by those who admire you? What story do you want someone else to tell about you?

We all need to be more kind to ourselves. It can be especially difficult when you're feeling low and stressed out. An easy self-care hack is to treat yourself the same way you would treat a good friend. Here are some tips:

- **Say good things about yourself.**
- **Cheer for yourself. You deserve good things.**
- **Plan a relaxing day to unwind and recharge.**
- **Be patient and understanding when you fuck up.**
- **Give yourself the same love you give to others.**
- **Read the last one again, bitch. YOU deserve that love.**

BE KIND TO YOURSELF

BE KIND TO YOUR BODY

Life is too short to waste any of it hating the way you look. Take some extra time in the mirror and write down all the things you appreciate about your body.

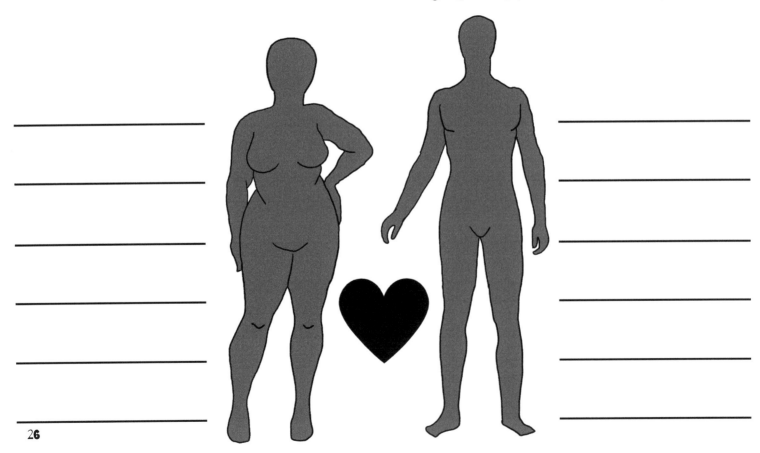

_____

_____

_____

_____

_____

_____

_____

_____

_____

_____

In case you forgot...

You do not have to do anything that makes you feel uncomfortable or doesn't serve the life you're building.

You can say no to anyone or anything at any time.

You decide what is best for you.

SELF CARE CHECKLIST

- ☐ Listen to your favorite album
- ☐ Take a relaxing bath
- ☐ Take a dance or cardio class
- ☐ Spend some time in nature
- ☐ Create something beautiful
- ☐ Make yourself a healthy meal
- ☐ Organize or clean something
- ☐ Go for a walk or a jog
- ☐ Plan a special day with a friend

- ☐ Embrace daily meditation
- ☐ Wake up early for the sunset
- ☐ Treat yourself to a favorite dessert
- ☐ Buy yourself a bouquet of flowers
- ☐ Take a mental health day
- ☐ Watch a movie from your childhood
- ☐ Spend time with cuddly animals
- ☐ Play a game or complete a puzzle
- ☐ Take a technology break

Make your own checklist

What activities are uniquely you? Create your own list of things that make you feel relaxed, loved, and refreshed.

- [ ] _____
- [ ] _____
- [ ] _____
- [ ] _____
- [ ] _____
- [ ] _____
- [ ] _____
- [ ] _____

Try to make these activities a monthly habit.

2

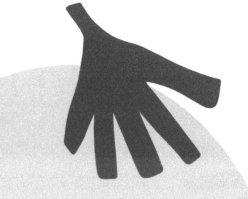

YOUR
BADASS
FUTURE

FIRST, MAKE TIME

It doesn't matter where you're at on your journey to happiness. What matters is that you start working toward it now. **And by now, I mean today, bitch!**

If you feel overwhelmed, just do a little at a time. For the first week, spend 10 minutes per day on a happiness activity. Set a timer and don't let anything distract you. If you get interrupted, start the time over again. Give it your all.

WEEK 1: 10 minutes a day   **WEEK 3:** 20 minutes a day

WEEK 2: 15 minutes a day   **WEEK 4:** 25 minutes a day

When you begin the next week, add an extra 5 minutes to your happiness habit. Repeat the process weekly. At the end of the month, you will have dedicated 8 hours to being happier. That's an entire workday! The more energy you devote to being happy, the better you will feel. That's a win!

HAPPINESS THROUGH
REMEMBERING

Take time out to enjoy a happy memory. Try to remember as much detail as possible. Reminiscing often can boost your mood and help you cope with stress. What are your top three favorite memories? Write down a prompt for each one. Revisit a memory once a week.

1.

2.

3.

Did you know that most people actually get more joy from looking forward to a special event -- like a vacation or party -- than they do from the event itself? The longer you get to look forward to something, the happier you will be.

Your event: _____

Event date: _____

LOOK FORWARD TO SOMETHING

DON'T BE A DICK!
BE GRATEFUL

When you take time out to focus on what you are thankful for, you get a boost of happiness. Practicing gratitude is a simple, low-effort method for increasing positive feelings and positive thoughts.

Make gratitude part of your routine

- Pick a day of the week to set aside some quiet time.
- Spend 10-15 minutes to write down what you're thankful for.
- Focus on a different area of your life each week, like career, health, family, etc. This will keep you from getting bored or listing the same things.
- Flip to the planner section of this workbook or keep a gratitude journal.
- Look back on your lists when you're having a hard day.

Let's start now!

What are you grateful for? Circle one:

Family   Career   Health   Friends   Love   Education   Art   Nature

Now set a timer and write about good things until it buzzes.

As you develop a habit of being grateful and focusing on good things in your life, you can shine that light outward as well. Start being vocal when you notice something positive about the people around you. Make an effort to slow down and give genuine recognition to your friends, family, and co-workers.

CONNECTION & RECOGNITION

Encouraging words can go a long way. Gratitude and recognition strengthen your connection with and appreciation for another person. Think about the last week. Is there someone you could have connected with by acknowledging a good deed or a job well done? Is it too late to thank them? Make a note:

_____

_____

_____

MEDITATE & QUIET YOUR MIND

When you make meditation a part of your routine, you can change the way you react to stress and anxiety.

Not only that, but meditating can actually change your brain. It can increase your grey matter and create new neural pathways, or connections, if you make it a daily habit.

Never tried meditation before? That's cool. Start small. Set aside 10 minutes after you wake up or before you go to bed.

Sit down, make yourself comfy, close your eyes. Stay quiet and still. Breathe.

Having a positive outlook can keep you healthier and happier. People who are optimistic live longer, are more productive, and have stronger relationships.

Optimism isn't about ignoring the bad stuff or being lucky. It's about changing the way you look at things.

So, how do you look on the bright side of a shitty situation?

OPTIMISM

This, too, shall pass.
Bad things are just temporary.

Things happen. It's not my fault.

PESSIMISM

This is how life is going to be now.

I did this. This is happening because of me.

PUT POSITIVITY INTO PRACTICE

Shitty experience I've had	Give it an optimistic spin

Can't shake the negativity? Flip to the back of the workbook.

Try to do something kind at least once a week. You can flip to the planner pages and plan it out. Or you can wait to be inspired. Think about how you can incorporate giving into your life.

Where would you run into someone who could use a hand? What could you do to put a smile on a friend, co-worker, or classmate's face? Write down your thoughts.

MAKE KINDNESS A ROUTINE

FORGIVE & LET GO

Another effective way to increase your happiness is to forgive others who have wronged you and give people grace. When you are able to show compassion instead of holding onto a grudge, you can reduce your stress level, lower your blood pressure, and improve your relationships.

Think about someone who treated you like shit. Now try to empathize with their mindset or what they have experienced in life. You don't have to agree with them, but write a letter and forgive them.

Dear _____ ,

_____

_____

_____

_____

_____

_____

_____

_____

NOW GIVE YOURSELF
THAT SAME GRACE

Give yourself the same forgiveness and understanding that you gave someone who has wronged you. No one can be perfect or take all the right steps. Think about the big mistakes you've made. What are you holding onto? What makes you dislike yourself? Dig deep. Now, forgive yourself.

Dear me,

_____

_____

_____

_____

_____

_____

_____

GET OUT OF YOUR COMFORT ZONE

Trying new things can boost positive emotions and reduce negativity. If you are willing to be bad at something, you'll start looking at failure in a different way. So go ahead and try!

- ☐ Wake up early on your days off
- ☐ Ask someone new to grab coffee
- ☐ Write a poem or a song
- ☐ Wear something bold or bright
- ☐ Take yourself out to a nice dinner
- ☐ Volunteer an hour of your time
- ☐ Start a conversation with a stranger
- ☐ Watch a genre of film you dislike
- ☐ Try a new hairstyle or new hair color

- ☐ Take a different route to work
- ☐ Buy new sheets or new shampoo
- ☐ Eat a new item off the lunch menu
- ☐ Fix something that is broken
- ☐ Visit a new city for a day
- ☐ Sign up for a class or workshop
- ☐ Rearrange your furniture
- ☐ Shop at a different grocery store
- ☐ Try a new sport or exercise routine

BRAINSTORM:

What else can you do to have new experiences?

10 YEARS FROM NOW

It's time to imagine your very best self. Forget about the things that are limiting you right now. Money? Job? Relationship? Degree? Location? Fitness? Skills? Let's take a moment to pretend that you have everything you want and you are living your dream life.

Where do you live?

What's your house like?

What is your job? How are you making money?

How are you contributing to the world or your community? How are you connecting to others?

What are your hobbies? Do you travel? Do you craft? Do you play sports? How do you relax?

What about a partner? What qualities does that person have? How do they make you feel?

What is your family like? Do you have close relationships? Kids? Grandkids? Pets? Parties?

What is your circle of friends like? How do you spend time and celebrate together?

How do you feel about your body? When you look in a mirror, what do you think?

Describe your perfect day. How do you feel? What are you doing?

WHAT A BEAUTIFUL LIFE!

If you didn't already realize it, you just started a ten-year plan. Hopefully, you listed out some big dreams and lovely things that you want in your life. Guess what, bitch? Now it's time to start thinking critically about how to get there.

On the following pages, you are going to break down your dreams into smaller goals. Goals are great tools to improve your self-esteem, give yourself something to work toward, and boost your feelings of success and accomplishment.

Think about who you want to be and how you want to feel in ten years. What goals could you make to get you there?

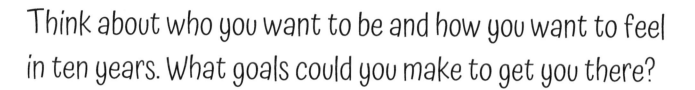

TURN DREAMS INTO ACHIEVABLE GOALS

BECOMING YOUR VERY BEST SELF

Decide on four major goals you can work on over the next few years. Don't be afraid to think big!

1 Describe your goal:

What needs to change for you to achieve this goal? What kind of mindset do you need?

2 Describe your goal:

What needs to change for you to achieve this goal? What kind of mindset do you need?

3 Describe your goal:

What needs to change for you to achieve this goal? What kind of mindset do you need?

4 Describe your goal:

What needs to change for you to achieve this goal? What kind of mindset do you need?

Great work! Now we're going to break your goals down into actions.

TURN GOALS INTO WORKABLE ACTIONS

1 List out all the actions you need to take to make this goal a reality:

Get specific and list as many actions as you can. Include even the smallest steps, like buying a notebook so you can start journaling or getting an application for a passport. If you are not sure about what needs to be done, look it up. A quick search can get rid of the mystery.

2 List out all the actions you need to take to make this goal a reality:

HAVING GOALS GIVES US MEANING AND PURPOSE

3 List out all the actions you need to take to make this goal a reality:

Making progress toward your goals makes you happier. When you feel that positive emotion, you are more likely to continue moving forward and trying to complete your goals.

4 **List out all the actions you need to take to make this goal a reality:**

Writing down exactly what it will take to achieve your dreams and goals can help make them feel more obtainable. All you have to do is start where you are and make a plan.

SUCCESS IS WAITING FOR YOU. YOU'VE GOT THIS!

THE NEXT 90 DAYS

You should be proud of yourself. You've already done the hard part of turning your goals into potential actions. Now you can use your list of action items as a road map for reaching each goal.

Use the calendar pages to plan out the next three months. You can focus on one goal at a time or tackle multiple goals at once. Experiment with it. Choose the rhythm that feels best for you.

What are the first steps you need to take? Start small. Mix in some other happiness strategies, like gratitude, connecting with others, remembering happy moments, and being kind to yourself.

LOOK AHEAD

PLAN YOUR MONTH

This month, my action items are:

WHICH GOAL?

- [ ] _____ 1 2 3 4
- [ ] _____ 1 2 3 4
- [ ] _____ 1 2 3 4
- [ ] _____ 1 2 3 4
- [ ] _____ 1 2 3 4
- [ ] _____ 1 2 3 4
- [ ] _____ 1 2 3 4
- [ ] _____ 1 2 3 4

This month, I will take care of myself by:

1. _____
2. _____
3. _____

I will be proactive & spend time with:

1. _____
2. _____
3. _____

	I'm grateful for:	My secret act of giving:	My happy memory:
WEEK 1			
WEEK 2			
WEEK 3			
WEEK 4			

S	M	T	W	T	F	S

LOOK AHEAD

This month, my action items are:

WHICH GOAL?

- [ ] _____ 1 2 3 4
- [ ] _____ 1 2 3 4
- [ ] _____ 1 2 3 4
- [ ] _____ 1 2 3 4
- [ ] _____ 1 2 3 4
- [ ] _____ 1 2 3 4
- [ ] _____ 1 2 3 4
- [ ] _____ 1 2 3 4

PLAN YOUR MONTH

This month, I will take care of myself by:

1. _____
2. _____
3. _____

I will be proactive & spend time with:

1. _____
2. _____
3. _____

	I'm grateful for:	My secret act of giving:	My happy memory:
WEEK 1			
WEEK 2			
WEEK 3			
WEEK 4			

S	M	T	W	T	F	S

63

LOOK AHEAD

PLAN YOUR MONTH

This month, my action items are:

- [ ] _____ 1 2 3 4
- [ ] _____ 1 2 3 4
- [ ] _____ 1 2 3 4
- [ ] _____ 1 2 3 4
- [ ] _____ 1 2 3 4
- [ ] _____ 1 2 3 4
- [ ] _____ 1 2 3 4
- [ ] _____ 1 2 3 4

This month, I will take care of myself by:

1. _____
2. _____
3. _____

I will be proactive & spend time with:

1. _____
2. _____
3. _____

	I'm grateful for:	My secret act of giving:	My happy memory:
WEEK 1			
WEEK 2			
WEEK 3			
WEEK 4			

S	M	T	W	T	F	S

65

NOW YOU'RE THREE MONTHS CLOSER TO YOUR GOALS!

Congratulations! Do you feel like a badass yet? Let's reflect on the last 90 days of working toward your goals and trying to be happier.

Did you complete all of your action items?   YES   NO

Which goal did you make the most progress on? Why?

What about the least amount of progress? Why?

How do you feel about the progress you've made overall?

ANOTHER 90-DAY SESSION

Now you can take the lessons you've learned and incorporate them into the next 90-day stretch. Set yourself up for success by being flexible and creating realistic expectations. You're on the right track!

What barriers are in the way of your goals or action items?

How can you be more successful during the next three months?

LOOK AHEAD

This month, my action items are:

- ☐ _____ 1 2 3 4
- ☐ _____ 1 2 3 4
- ☐ _____ 1 2 3 4
- ☐ _____ 1 2 3 4
- ☐ _____ 1 2 3 4
- ☐ _____ 1 2 3 4
- ☐ _____ 1 2 3 4
- ☐ _____ 1 2 3 4

PLAN YOUR MONTH

This month, I will take care of myself by:

1. _____
2. _____
3. _____

I will be proactive & spend time with:

1. _____
2. _____
3. _____

	I'm grateful for:	My secret act of giving:	My happy memory:
WEEK 1			
WEEK 2			
WEEK 3			
WEEK 4			

S	M	T	W	T	F	S

LOOK AHEAD

This month, my action items are:

WHICH GOAL?

- ☐ _____ 1 2 3 4
- ☐ _____ 1 2 3 4
- ☐ _____ 1 2 3 4
- ☐ _____ 1 2 3 4
- ☐ _____ 1 2 3 4
- ☐ _____ 1 2 3 4
- ☐ _____ 1 2 3 4
- ☐ _____ 1 2 3 4

PLAN YOUR MONTH

This month, I will take care of myself by:

1. _____
2. _____
3. _____

I will be proactive & spend time with:

1. _____
2. _____
3. _____

	I'm grateful for:	My secret act of giving:	My happy memory:
WEEK 1			
WEEK 2			
WEEK 3			
WEEK 4			

S	M	T	W	T	F	S

LOOK AHEAD

PLAN YOUR MONTH

This month, my action items are:

WHICH GOAL?

☐ _____ 1 2 3 4

☐ _____ 1 2 3 4

☐ _____ 1 2 3 4

☐ _____ 1 2 3 4

☐ _____ 1 2 3 4

☐ _____ 1 2 3 4

☐ _____ 1 2 3 4

☐ _____ 1 2 3 4

This month, I will take care of myself by:

1. _____

2. _____

3. _____

I will be proactive & spend time with:

1. _____

2. _____

3. _____

	I'm grateful for:	My secret act of giving:	My happy memory:
WEEK 1			
WEEK 2			
WEEK 3			
WEEK 4			

S	M	T	W	T	F	S

WHERE ARE YOU NOW, BITCH?

	The worst	Meh	The best
MOOD			
ENERGY			
HEALTH			
CAREER			
FINANCES			
GROWTH			
FAMILY			
LOVE LIFE			
SOCIAL			

You made it happen!

What is today's date? _____

When did you start? _____

How do you feel about your progress?

_____

_____

_____

Describe what your life is like now in six words:

_____   _____   _____

_____   _____   _____

Wow! You should be so proud of yourself. Look back at the first pages
of this workbook and reflect on how far you have come. Be impressed.

REWARD YOURSELF

Now it's time to celebrate! It's really important to take time to honor your successes and reward yourself for the hard work.

How are you going to celebrate?

What about your next reward? Think about what your next celebration will be. Then get to work on that next set of action items and goals.

You are so ready, bitch!

NEGATIVITY
IS BULLSHIT

GO AHEAD AND VENT

Reflecting can be healthy. Get it out.

JUST DON'T DWELL HERE

FUCK THESE THOUGHTS

EVERYTHING IS TEMPORARY,
ESPECIALLY FEELING LIKE SHIT.

Finished? Good.
Now tear out these
pages and burn them.

It is incredibly easy to find fault in yourself when you experience rejection. We turn ourselves into punching bags the moment someone cancels a date or does not respond to a text. But is it really about us? Nope. Turn rejection around and realize it's not about you.

REJECTION ISN'T ABOUT YOU

When someone does not choose you, it's not about what unique qualities you have to offer. You are just not a good fit for what they want. It's time to realize that's ok! We can't all be perfect for each other or perfect for every job.

In fact, we often feel the same way about people who express their interest in us. Be honest. You have a specific kind of person in mind, too. There is nothing wrong with that. The issues arise when you let rejection affect your self-esteem.

NEGATIVE THOUGHT CYCLES

What we think has a profound effect on how we feel and how we act. When we get pulled into a negative frame of mind, it can quickly spiral out of control.

Have you ever noticed how one shitty thing can ruin your day? With a better understanding of the negative thought cycle, you can learn how to stop it.

Negative thought
My friends don't really care

Negative behavior
Canceling plans, being hostile

Negative emotion
Doubt, sadness, resentment

IDENTIFY THE PATTERNS

Think of a recent time when your thoughts spiraled into negativity. How did it affect your emotions? How did it change your actions? Write it out.

How could have a less negative thought affected your actions and mood?

Your negative thought

Your negative behavior

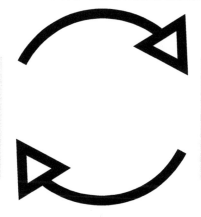

Your negative emotion

INTERRUPT THE CYCLE

You don't have to be stuck in a cycle of negative thoughts. You can interrupt the negativity and pull yourself out of the spiral.

Make a list of positive things that you know are true. For example: "My best friend loves me" or "I'm really good at baking."

Next time negativity starts to take over, revisit this list. Tell yourself to stop thinking negative thoughts. Read the positive truths to yourself or say them out loud.

Positive truths about me

Insert these truths into a negative thought cycle to break out of the bullshit.

BE **HAPPY**, BITCH!

Find more resources and a community of amazing people
getting happier and healthier at www.behappybitch.com

REFERENCES

Gratitude

Armenta, C. N., Fritz, M. M., & Lyubomirsky, S. (2017). "Functions of Positive Emotions." Emotion Review, 9(3), 183–190.

Algoe, S. B., & Stanton, A. L. (2012). "Gratitude when it is needed most." Emotion, 12(1), 163–168.

Davis, D. E., Choe, E., Meyers, et all. (2015). "Thankful for the Little Things." Journal of Counseling Psychology, 63(1), 20–31.

Positivity and optimism

Chambers, R., Gullone, E., & Allen, N. B. (2009). "Mindful emotion regulation" Clinical Psychology Review, 29(6), 560–572.

Fredrickson, B. L. (2001). "The role of positive emotions." The American Psychologist, 56(3), 218–226.

McRae, K., & Mauss, I. B. (2016). "Increasing Positive Emotion." In Positive Neuroscience (pp. 159–174). Oxford University Press.

Goal setting and progress

Deci, Edward L. and Ryan, Richard M. (2000). "The What and Why of Goal Pursuits." Psychological Inquiry. 11:4, pp. 227-268,

Hennecke M., Brandstätter V. (2017) "Means, Ends, and Happiness." Robinson M., Eid M. (eds) The Happy Mind. Springer, Cham.

Giving and kindness

Borgonovi, F. (2008). "Doing well by doing good." Social Science and Medicine, 66(11), 2321–2334.

Jenkinson, C. E., Dickens, A. P., et al. (2013). "Is volunteering a public health intervention?" BMC Public Health, 13(1), 773.

Koo, M., & Fishbach, A. (2016). "Giving the Self." Social Psychological and Personality Science, 7(4), 339–348.

Happiness

Abram, M., Picard, L., Navarro, B. (2014). "Mechanisms of remembering the past." Consciousness and Cognition, 29(1), 76–89.

Lyubomirsky, Sonja, Laura King. 2005."Does happiness lead to success?" Psychological Bulletin 131, no. 6:803–55

O'Brien, Catherine (2012). "Sustainable happiness and well-being." Psychology. 3:12A, pp. 1196–1201.

Forgiveness

Robert D. Enright. "The Forgiving Life." Washington, DC: American Psychological Association, 2012.

Witvliet, C.V.O., Ludwig, T. E., (2001). "Granting forgiveness of harboring grudges." Psychological Science, 12, 117-123.